SPEAK ANOTHER LANGUAGE!

MY FIRST RUSSIAN PHRASES

BY
JILL KALZ
ILLUSTRATED BY
DANIELE FABBRI
TRANSLATED BY
TRANSLATIONS.COM

PICTURE WINDOW BOOKS
a capstone imprint

TABLE OF
CONTENTS

HOW TO USE THIS DICTIONARY

This book is full of useful phrases in both English and Russian. The English phrase appears first, followed by the Russian phrase. Look below each Russian phrase for help to sound it out. Try reading the phrases aloud.

Topic heading in English

Topic heading in Russian

Additional phrases to learn

Phrase in English
Phrase in Russian
(pronunciation)

English: THE BASICS

Russian: ОБЩИЕ ФРАЗЫ (OB-shchiyeh fr-AH-zy)

Hello.
Привет.
(pree-VYET)

Excuse me.
Извини.
(eez-vee-NEE)

Good-bye.
Пока.
(puh-KAH)

Please.
Пожалуйста.
(puh-ZHAH-loo-stuh)

Good morning.
Доброе утро.
(DOH-bro-yeh OO-truh)

Good afternoon.
Добрый день.
(DOH-bree dyen')

Good night.
Спокойной ночи.
(spah-KOY-nay NO-chee)

What is your name?
Как тебя зовут?
(kahk teb-YA zah-VOOT)

Thank you.
Спасибо.
(spa-SEE-buh)

You are welcome.
Не за что.
(NYE za shtoh)

My name is ___.
Меня зовут ___.
(men-YA zah-VOOT ___)

MORE TO LEARN

Yes
да
(da)

No
нет
(nyet)

6

NOTES ABOUT THE RUSSIAN LANGUAGE

In this book you may see two ways to say a phrase. Some Russian words change form, depending on whether a man or woman says them. They may also change depending on the person to whom or about whom you are speaking. If you are male, or asking a man a question or talking about a man, use the first way. If you are female, or asking a woman a question or talking about a woman, use the second way.

Most consonants in the Russian language can be either "hard" or "soft." An apostrophe (') in the Russian pronunciations signals that the letter before it is soft. Soften a consonant by touching your tongue to the roof of your mouth.

3

LETTERS OF THE ALPHABET
AND THEIR PRONUNCIATIONS

А а • ah	Б б • beh	В в • veh
Г г • geh	Д д • deh	Е е • yeh
Ё ё • yoh	Ж ж • zheh	З з • zeh
И и • ee	Й й • ee kr-AHT-ka-yeh (И краткое: short ee)	К к • kah
Л л • el	М м • em	Н н • en
О о • oh	П п • peh	Р р • ehr
С с • es	Т т • teh	У у • oo
Ф ф • eff	Х х • hah	Ц ц • tseh
Ч ч • cheh	Ш ш • shah	Щ щ • schyah
ъ • tv-YOR-di znak (твёрдый знак: hard sign)	ы • eigh	ь • MYAH-kee znak (мягкий знак: soft sign)
Э э • eh	Ю ю • yoo	Я я • yah

IT SOUNDS LIKE

There are 33 letters in the Russian (or Cyrillic) alphabet. Many of the letters sound like English letters. But some don't. The Russian letter ы, for example, doesn't exist in English. Use this guide to learn how to say these sounds.

	LETTER	SOUND	PRONUNCIATION	EXAMPLES	
CONSONANTS	б	b	like b in box	буфет	boof-YET
	в	v	like v in very, but sometimes like f at the beginning of a word	весна вчера	vyes-NAH fcher-AH
	г	g	like g in good, but like k at the end of a word	голова четверг	guh-luh-VAH cheht-VYERK
	д	d	like d in day	день	dyen'
	ж	zh	like s in measure	живу	zhee-VOO
	з	z	like z in zoo	завтрак	ZAHV-truhk
	к	k	like c in car	кошка	KOHSH-kuh
	л	l	like l in like	лето	LYET-uh
	м	m	like m in may	март	mart
	н	n	like n in no	нет	nyet
	п	p	like p in pie	пять	pyat'
	р	r	like r in proud, but slightly rolled	брат	braht
	с	s	like s in say	спасибо	spa-SEE-buh
	т	t	like t in toy	ты	tih
	ф	f	like f in fun	фильм	feel'm
	х	kh	like ch in Loch Ness (sounds like you are clearing your throat)	холодно	KHOH-lud-nuh
	ц	ts	like ts in cats	отец	uh-TYETS
	ч	ch	like ch in cheese, but like sh before a consonant	четверг что	chet-VYERK shtoh
	ш	sh	like sh in fresh	шапка	SHAHP-kuh
	щ	shch	like sh in fresh, as said with a wide smile	щенок	shchen-OHK
VOWELS	а	a	like a in car when stressed, like u in butter when not stressed	знаю мама	ZNAH-yoo MAH-muh
	е	ye	like ye in yet	есть	yest'
	ё	yo	like yo in yogurt	тетя	TYO-tyuh
	и	ee	like e in we	напиток	nah-PEE-tuhk
	о	o	like o in home when stressed, like u in butter or a in about when not stressed	что утро обед	shtoh OO-truh ah-BYED
	у	oo	like oo in boot	ужин	OO-zhin
	ы	ih	like i in it, but with your tongue lower in your mouth	ты	tih
	э	eh	like e in bed	это	EH-tuh
	ю	yu	like the word you	июнь	ee-YOON'
	я	ya	like ya in yard	я	yah
VOWEL COMBINATIONS	ай	ai	like i in hi	китайский	kee-TAI-skee
	ой	oi	like oy in boy	твой	tvoy
	ей	ay	like ay in way	клей	klay
	яй	yai	like yi in yikes	яйцо	yai-TSOH
SPECIAL LETTERS	й	ee	Called "short ee," the letter follows other vowels to make vowel combinations.		
	ь	soft sign	The soft sign has no sound of its own. It softens the sound of the consonant before it.		
	ъ	hard sign	The hard sign has no sound of its own. It keeps the consonant before it hard.		

English: THE BASICS

Hello.
Привет.
(pree-VYET)

Good morning.
Доброе утро.
(DOH-bro-yeh OO-truh)

Good afternoon.
Добрый день.
(DOH-bree dyen')

Good night.
Спокойной ночи.
(spoh-KOY-noy NO-chee)

Excuse me.
Извини.
(eez-vee-NEE)

Good-bye.
Пока.
(puh-KAH)

Please.
Пожалуйста.
(puh-ZHAH-loo-stuh)

Russian: ОБЩИЕ ФРАЗЫ (OB-shchee-yeh fr-AH-zih)

Thank you.
Спасибо.
(spa-SEE-buh)

You are welcome.
Не за что.
(NYE za shtoh)

What is your name?
Как тебя зовут?
(kahk teb-YA zah-VOOT)

My name is ____.
Меня зовут ___.
(men-YA zah-VOOT ___)

MORE TO LEARN

Yes	No
да	**нет**
(da)	(nyet)

7

Russian: КТО ТЫ? (ktoh tih)

How old are you?
Сколько тебе лет?
(SKOHL'-kuh teb-YEH lyet)

I am __ years old.
Мне __ лет.
(men-YEH __ lyet)

I have a pet bird.
У меня есть домашнее животное — птица.
(oo men-YA yest' doh-MASH-ne-ye zhee-VOHT-no-yeh — puh-TEE-tsuh)

It does tricks.
Она умеет выполнять трюки.
(uh-NAH oom-YAY-et vih-poln-YAHT' tr-YOO-kee)

dog
собака
(suh-BAH-kuh)

cat
кошка
(KOHSH-kuh)

11

Are you hungry?
Ты хочешь есть?
(tih KHOH-chesh' yest')

I am hungry.
Я хочу есть.
(ya khuh-CHOO yest')

I am thirsty.
Я хочу пить.
(ya khuh-CHOO peet')

What is for supper?
Что на ужин?
(shtoh nah OO-zhin)

lunch
обед
(ah-BYED)

breakfast
завтрак
(ZAHF-truhk)

MORE TO LEARN

I am not hungry.
Я не хочу есть.
(ya nyeh khuh-CHOO yest')

Russian: СЕМЬЯ (sem'-YA)

Do you speak English?
Ты говоришь по-английски?
(tih guh-vuh-REESH' puh-ahn-GLEE-skee)

Chinese
по-китайски
(puh-kee-TAI-skee)

French
по-французски
(puh-frahn-TSOOZ-kee)

German
по-немецки
(puh-neh-MYETS-kee)

Spanish
по-испански
(puh-ees-PAHN-skee)

A little.
Немного.
(nyem-NO-guh)

MORE TO LEARN

my father	my sister	my brother
мой отец	**моя сестра**	**мой брат**
(moy uh-TYETS)	(mah-YA sis-TRAH)	(moy braht)

15

Russian: ДАТА И ВРЕМЯ (DAH-tuh ee VREM-ya)

Today is Saturday.
Сегодня суббота.
(seh-VOHD-nyah soo-BOH-tah)

Tomorrow is Sunday.
Завтра воскресенье.
(ZAF-trah vahs-kre-SEN'-yeh)

Yesterday was Friday.
Вчера была пятница.
(fcher-AH bih-LAH PYAHT-nee-tsah)

MORE TO LEARN

Sunday
воскресенье
(vahs-kre-SEN'-yeh)

Monday
понедельник
(puh-nee-DYEL'-neek)

Tuesday
вторник
(FTOR-neek)

Wednesday
среда
(sre-DAH)

Thursday
четверг
(chet-VYERK)

Friday
пятница
(PYAHT-nee-tsah)

Saturday
суббота
(soo-BOH-tah)

Russian: МЕСЯЦЫ И ВРЕМЕНА ГОДА

(MYES'-yah-tsih ee vre-myen-AH GO-dah)

I love summer!
Я люблю лето!
(ya loob-LYOO LYET-uh)

fall
осень
(OH-syen')

winter
зиму
(zee-MOO)

spring
весну
(vyes-NOO)

MORE TO LEARN

January
январь
(yahn-VAR')

February
февраль
(fev-RAHL')

March
март
(mart)

April
апрель
(ah-PREL')

May
май
(my)

June
июнь
(ee-YOON')

July
июль
(ee-YOOL')

August
август
(AHV-goost)

September
сентябрь
(sen-TYABR')

October
октябрь
(ahk-TYABR')

November
ноябрь
(nuh-YABR')

December
декабрь
(dyeh-KABR')

How is the weather?
Какая сегодня погода?
(kuh-KAH-ya seh-VOHD-nyah puh-GO-duh)

It is raining.
Идет дождь.
(eed-YOHT dohsht')

snowing
снег
(sn-YEK)

Don't forget an umbrella!
Не забудь зонтик!
(nye zah-BOOT' ZOHN-teek)

Russian: ПОГОДА (puh-GO-duh)

It is cold.
Сегодня холодно.
(seh-VOHD-nyah KHOH-lud-nuh)

hot
жарко
(ZHAR-kuh)

sunny
солнечно
(SOHL-nich-nuh)

Wear a coat.
Надень пальто.
(na-DYEN' pahl'-TOH)

a hat
шапку
(SHAHP-koo)

mittens
варежки
(VAR-yesh-kee)

boots
сапоги
(sah-puh-GEE)

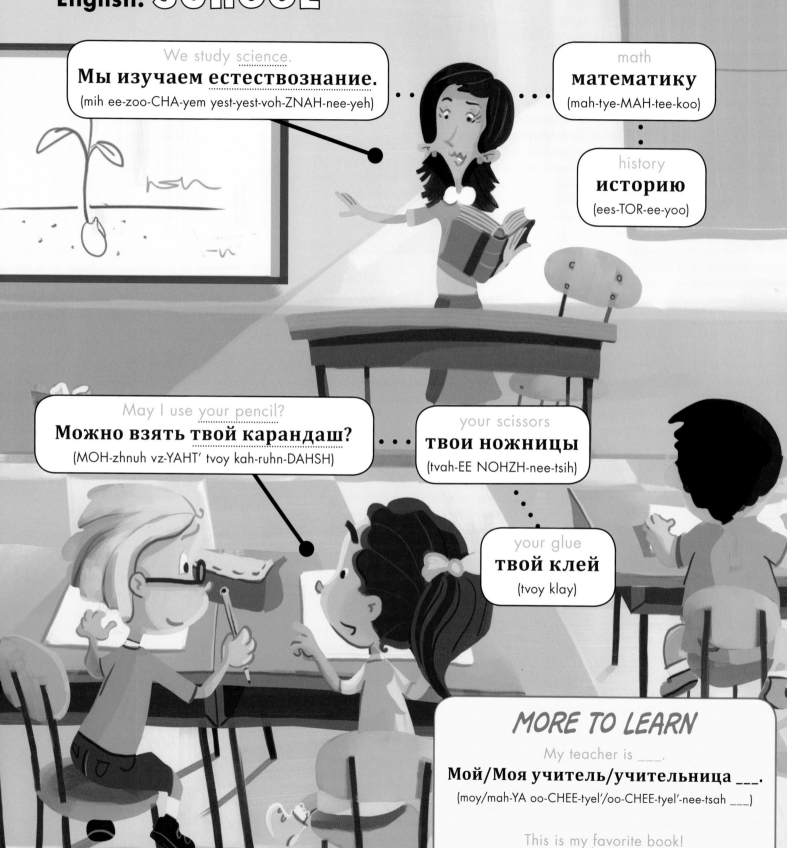

We study science.
Мы изучаем естествознание.
(mih ee-zoo-CHA-yem yest-yest-voh-ZNAH-nee-yeh)

math
математику
(mah-tye-MAH-tee-koo)

history
историю
(ees-TOR-ee-yoo)

May I use your pencil?
Можно взять твой карандаш?
(MOH-zhnuh vz-YAHT' tvoy kah-ruhn-DAHSH)

your scissors
твои ножницы
(tvah-EE NOHZH-nee-tsih)

your glue
твой клей
(tvoy klay)

MORE TO LEARN

My teacher is ___.
Мой/Моя учитель/учительница ___.
(moy/mah-YA oo-CHEE-tyel'/oo-CHEE-tyel'-nee-tsah ___)

This is my favorite book!
Это моя любимая книга!
(EH-tuh mah-YA lyoo-BEE-mah-yah kuh-NEE-guh)

Russian: ШКОЛА (SHKOH-luh)

Where is the bathroom?
Где здесь туалет?
(guh-DYEH zdyes' too-ah-LYET)

lunchroom
буфет
(boof-YET)

bus stop
автобусная остановка
(ahf-TOH-boos-nah-ya ah-stah-NOHF-kuh)

Go right.
Идите направо.
(ee-DEE-tye na-PRA-vuh)

left
налево
(nah-LYE-vuh)

straight ahead
прямо
(pr-YA-muh)

Are you ready for the test?
Ты подготовился/подготовилась к зкзамену?
(tih puhd-guh-TOH-veel-sah/puhd-guh-TOH-veel-ahs' k ehk-ZAH-myen-oo)

I forgot.
Я забыл/забыла.
(ya za-BIHL/za-BIHL-uh)

Russian: ДОМА (DOH-mah)

What did you say?
Что ты сказал/сказала?
(shtoh tih ska-ZAHL/skah-ZAH-luh)

Mom is in the garage.
Мама в гараже.
(MAH-muh v gahr-ah-ZHEH)

Go outside.
Иди на улицу.
(EE-dee na OO-lee-tsoo)

upstairs
наверх
(na-VYERKH)

downstairs
вниз
(vnees)

English: HOBBIES

Do you play sports?
Ты занимаешься спортом?
(tih za-nee-MAH-yesh'-sya SPORT-uhm)

I play baseball.
Я играю в бейсбол.
(ya ee-GRAH-yoo v base-BOHL)

soccer
футбол
(foot-BOHL)

basketball
баскетбол
(bah-skyet-BOHL)

football
американский футбол
(ah-mer-ee-KAHN-skee foot-BOHL)

I won.
Я выиграл/выиграла.
(ya VIH-ee-grahl/VIH-ee-grahl-uh)

I lost.
Я проиграл/проиграла.
(ya pruh-ee-GRAHL/pruh-ee-GRAHL-uh)

Congratulations!
Поздравляю!
(puz-drahv-LYA-yoo)

Russian: ХОББИ (KHOH-bee)

What is your favorite book?
Какая твоя любимая книга?
(kuh-KAH-ya tvuh-YA lyoo-BEE-mah-ya kuh-NEE-guh)

NOVELS

TV show
телепередача
(tele-peh-reh-DAH-chah)

Who is your favorite male singer?
Кто твой любимый певец?
(kuh-TOH tvoy lyoo-BEE-mee pev-YETS)

What is your favorite movie?
Какой твой любимый фильм?
(kah-KOY tvoy lyoo-BEE-mee feel'm)

FILMS MOVIES

MORE TO LEARN

Good luck!
Удачи!
(oo-DA-chee)

Numbers • ЧИСЛА (CHEES-luh)

1 one • **один** (uh-DEEN)

2 two • **два** (dvah)

3 three • **три** (tree)

4 four • **четыре** (che-TEER-eh)

5 five • **пять** (pyat')

6 six • **шесть** (shest')

7 seven • **семь** (syem')

8 eight • **восемь** (VOH-syem')

9 nine • **девять** (DYEV-yaht')

10 ten • **десять** (DYES-yaht')

11 eleven • **одиннадцать** (uh-DEEN-nahd-tsaht')

12 twelve • **двенадцать** (dvyeh-NAHD-tsaht')

13 thirteen • **тринадцать** (tree-NAHD-tsaht')

14 fourteen • **четырнадцать** (che-TEER-nahd-tsaht')

15 fifteen • **пятнадцать** (pyat-NAHD-tsaht')

16 sixteen • **шестнадцать** (shest-NAHD-tsaht')

17 seventeen • **семнадцать** (syem-NAHD-tsaht')

18 eighteen • **восемнадцать** (voh-syem-NAHD-tsaht')

19 nineteen • **девятнадцать** (dyev-yaht-NAHD-tsaht')

20 twenty • **двадцать** (DVAD-tsaht')

30 thirty • **тридцать** (TREED-tsaht')

40 forty • **сорок** (SOH-ruhk)

50 fifty • **пятьдесят** (peet'-des-YAHT)

60 sixty • **шестьдесят** (shest'-des-YAHT)

70 seventy • **семьдесят** (syem'-des-YAHT)

80 eighty • **восемьдесят** (VOH-syem'-des-yaht)

90 ninety • **девяносто** (dev-yah-NOH-stuh)

100 one hundred • **сто** (stoh)

Colors • ЦВЕТА (tsveh-TAH)

 red • **красный**
(KRAHS-nee)

 purple • **фиолетовый**
(fee-ah-LYET-ah-vee)

 orange • **оранжевый**
(ah-RAHN-zhev-ee)

 pink • **розовый**
(ROH-zoh-vee)

 yellow • **желтый**
(ZHOL-tee)

 brown • **коричневый**
(kah-REECH-nye-vee)

 green • **зеленый**
(zel-YOH-nee)

 black • **черный**
(CHOR-nee)

 blue • **синий**
(SEE-nee)

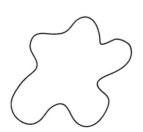 white • **белый**
(BYEL-ee)

READ MORE

Hunt, Jilly. *Russian.* Languages of the World. Chicago: Heinemann Library, 2012.

Kudela, Katy R. *My First Book of Russian Words.* Bilingual Picture Dictionaries. Mankato, Minn.: Capstone Press, 2010.

Melling, David, ill. *First Russian Words.* English words compiled by Neil Morris; Russian translation by Marcia Krisan. Oxford; New York: Oxford University Press, 2009.

INTERNET SITES

FactHound offers a safe, fun way to find Internet sites related to this book. All of the sites on FactHound have been researched by our staff.

Here's all you do:

Visit *www.facthound.com*

Type in this code: 9781404875159

 Super-cool stuff! Check out projects, games and lots more at www.capstonekids.com

LOOK FOR ALL THE BOOKS IN THE SPEAK ANOTHER LANGUAGE SERIES:

MY FIRST ARABIC *PHRASES*

MY FIRST FRENCH *PHRASES*

MY FIRST GERMAN *PHRASES*

MY FIRST ITALIAN *PHRASES*

MY FIRST JAPANESE *PHRASES*

MY FIRST MANDARIN CHINESE *PHRASES*

MY FIRST RUSSIAN *PHRASES*

MY FIRST SPANISH *PHRASES*

Set Designer: Alison Thiele
Production Designer: Eric Manske
Art Director: Nathan Gassman
Production Specialist: Laura Manthe
Language & Culture Consultant: Ksenia Kologrieva
The illustrations in this book were created digitally.

Picture Window Books
1710 Roe Crest Drive
North Mankato, Minnesota 56003
www.capstonepub.com

Library of Congress Cataloging-in-Publication Data
Kalz, Jill, author.
  My first Russian phrases / by Jill Kalz ; illustrations by Daniele Fabbri.
    pages : illustrations ; cm. — (Speak another language!)
  Audience: K to Grade 3.
  ISBN 978-1-4048-7515-9 (library binding)
  ISBN 978-1-4048-7740-5 (paperback)
  ISBN 978-1-4048-7998-0 (ebook pdf)
(print) 1. Russian language—Conversation and phrase books—English—Juvenile literature. I. Fabbri, Daniele, 1978–, illustrator. II. Title. III. Series: Speak another language!

  PG2121.K28 2013
  491.78'3421—dc23   2012008526

Printed in the United States of America in North Mankato, Minnesota.
042012   006682CGF12